Y0-CAR-291

Algrove Publishing Limited
1090 Morrison Drive
Ottawa, Ontario
Canada K2H 1C2

Canadian Cataloguing in Publication Data

Main entry under title:

A book of alphabets with plain, ornamental, ancient and mediaeval styles

(Classic reprint series)
Reprint, with original title pages, of A set of alphabets / drawn and arranged by Fred'k S. Copley. New York : G.E. Woodward, 1870, and, The book of ornamental alphabets / collected and engraved by F. Delamotte. London : Crosby Lockwood and Son, 1895.
Includes index.
ISBN 1-894572-08-4

1. Alphabets. 2. Printing--Specimens. 3. Lettering. I. Copley, Frederick S. Set of alphabets. II. Delamotte, F. (Freeman), 1814-1862. Book of ornamental alphabets. III. Series: Classic reprint series (Ottawa, Ont.)

NK3600.B65 2000 686.2'24 C00-900967-1

Printed in Canada
#21200

PUBLISHER'S NOTE

Copley's Plain & Ornamental Standard Alphabets was published in New York in 1870; *The Book of Ornamental Alphabets, Ancient and Mediaeval* (spelled just like that!) was published in London 25 years later. In some ways, they reflect their countries of origin. Copley's confidently instructs the reader in the use of diverse alphabets in constructing map and other titles, as well as tossing in odd bits of interesting filler. The British book hews more closely to the contents promised by the title, allowing no familiarity to creep in. There is little content overlap between the two. According to the ex libris embossings in the front of the copy of Copley's we reprinted from, it was variously owned by the Deep Sea Isinglass Company (1873), Odd Fellows' Mutual Benefit Association of Cape Ann, Massachusetts (also 1873) and finally the Rhode Island Locomotive Works of Providence (1878). Obviously there was a catholic interest in alphabets in that era.

Leonard G. Lee, Publisher
Ottawa
August 2000

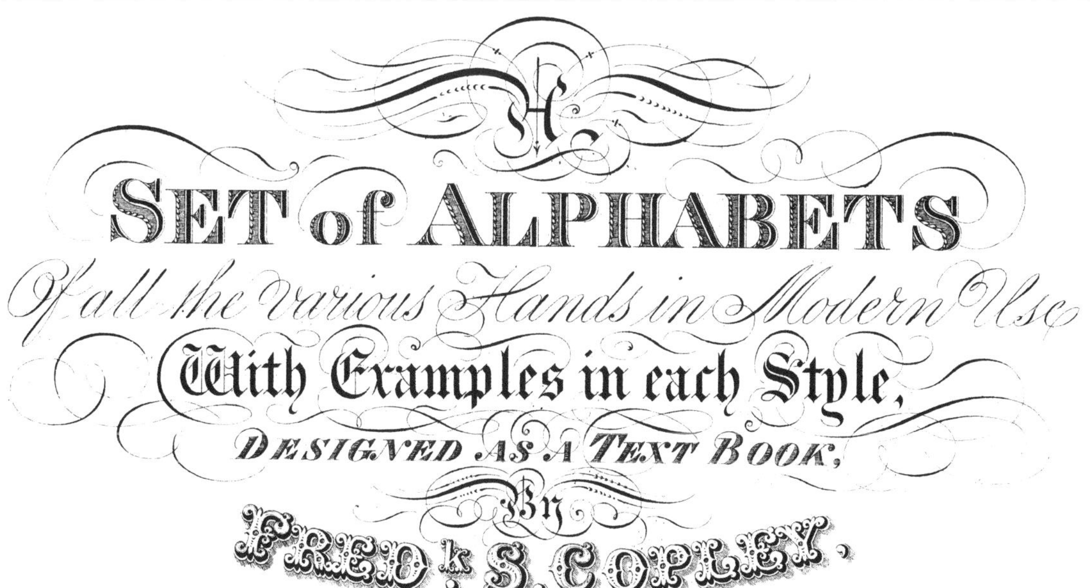

NEW YORK.

PUBLISHED By GEO. E. WOODWARD

191 BROADWAY.

Engraved by Korff Bro.s 54 William St.

A SET OF ALPHABETS

OF ALL THE VARIOUS HANDS OF MODERN USE.

With Examples in each Style.

ALSO, THE

Mechanical & Analytical Construction of Letters, Figures & Titles

WITH DESIGNS FOR

Titles, Ciphers, Monograms, Borders, Compasses, Flourishes, Etc.

DESIGNED AS A TEXT-BOOK FOR THE USE OF DRAUGHTSMEN, CIVIL ENGINEERS, SURVEYORS, ARCHITECTS, ENGRAVERS, DESIGNERS, SIGN PAINTERS, SCHOOLS, ETC.

Drawn and Arranged by Fred'k S. Copley.

NEW YORK:
GEO E. WOODWARD; ORANGE JUDD & CO., 245 BROADWAY.
ENGRAVED BY KORFF BROS., 54 WILLIAM STREET.

CONTENTS.

MECHANICAL METHOD OF CONSTRUCTING EGYPTIAN LETTERS AND FIGURES.

1 2 3 4 5 A B C D E F G H I J K L M N 1 2 3 4 5

1 2 3 4 5 1 2 3 4 5 6 7 8 9 0. 1 2 3 4 5

1 2 3 4 5 O P Q R S T U V W X Y Z. 1 2 3 4 5

MECHANICAL METHOD OF CONSTRUCTING BLOCK LETTERS AND FIGURES.

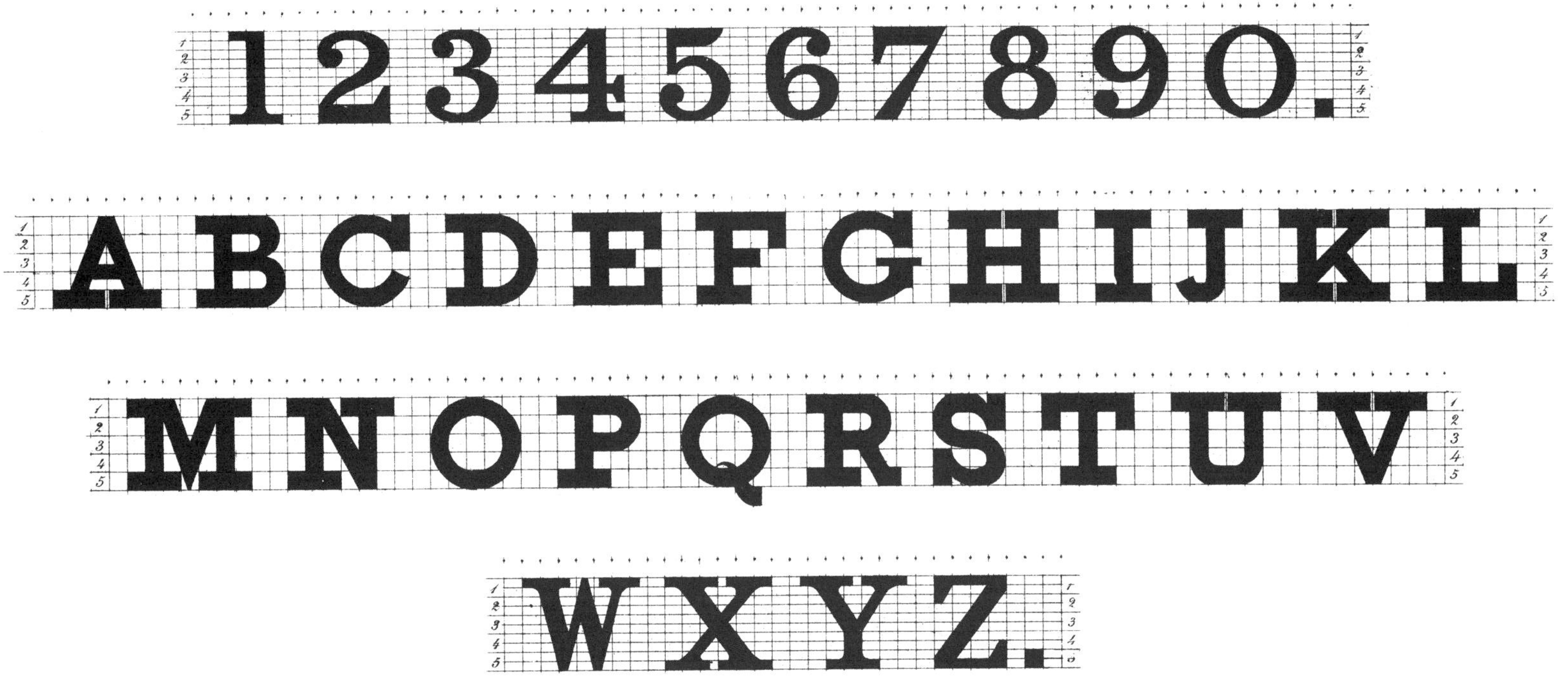

1 2 3 4 5 6 7 8 9 0.

A B C D E F G H I J K L

M N O P Q R S T U V

W X Y Z.

MECHANICAL METHOD OF CONSTRUCTING ROMAN LETTERS AND FIGURES.

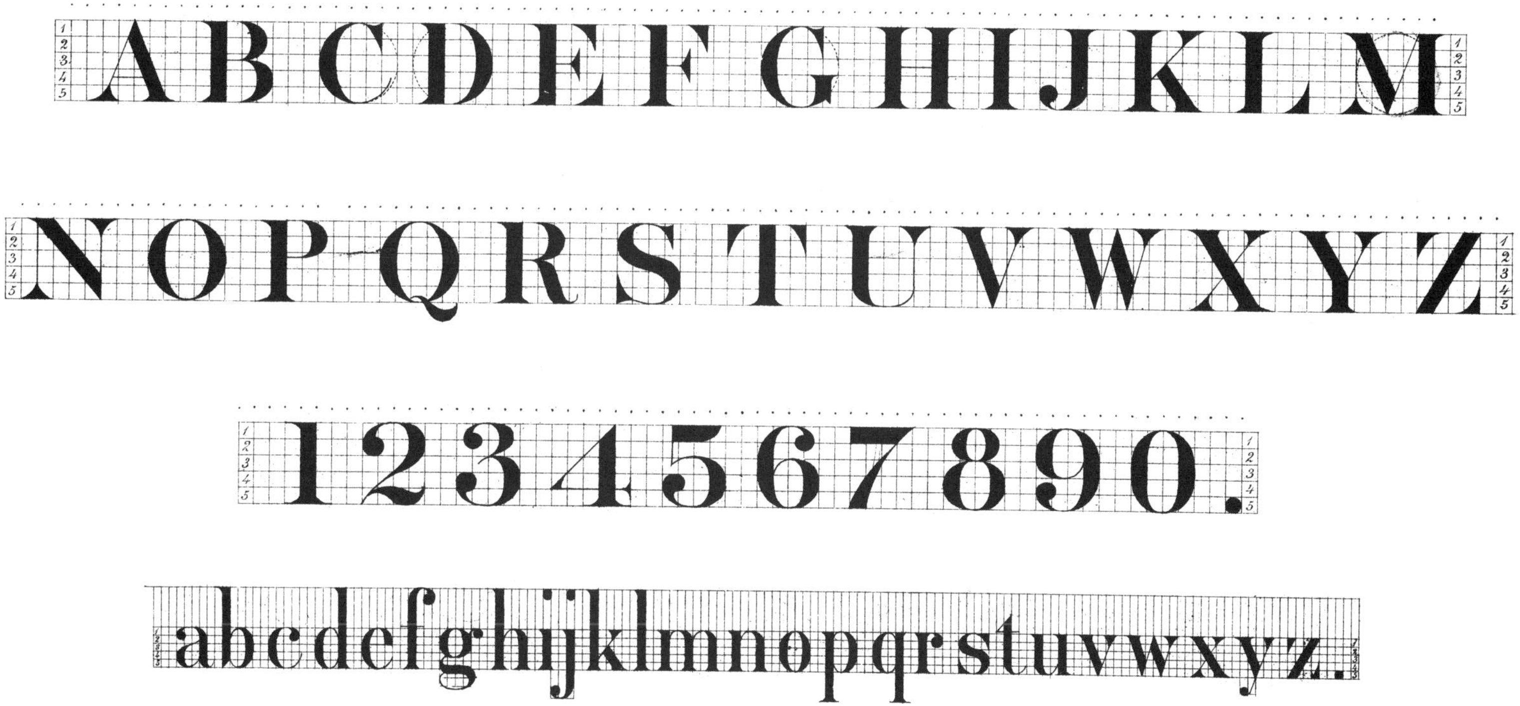

1 2 3 4 5 A B C D E F G H I J K L M 1 2 3 4 5

1 2 3 4 5 N O P Q R S T U V W X Y Z 1 2 3 4 5

1 2 3 4 5 1 2 3 4 5 6 7 8 9 0. 1 2 3 4 5

1 2 3 4 5 a b c d e f g h i j k l m n o p q r s t u v w x y z. 1 2 3 4 5

MECHANICAL METHOD OF CONSTRUCTING ITALIC LETTERS AND FIGURES.

1 2 3 4 5 *A B C D E F G H I J K L M* 1 2 3 4 5

1 2 3 4 5 *N O P Q R S T U V W X Y Z.* 1 2 3 4 5

1 2 3 4 5 *1 2 3 4 5 6 7 8 9 0.* 1 2 3 4 5

abcdefghijklmnopqrstuvwxyz.

ANALYTICAL ROMAN LARGE.

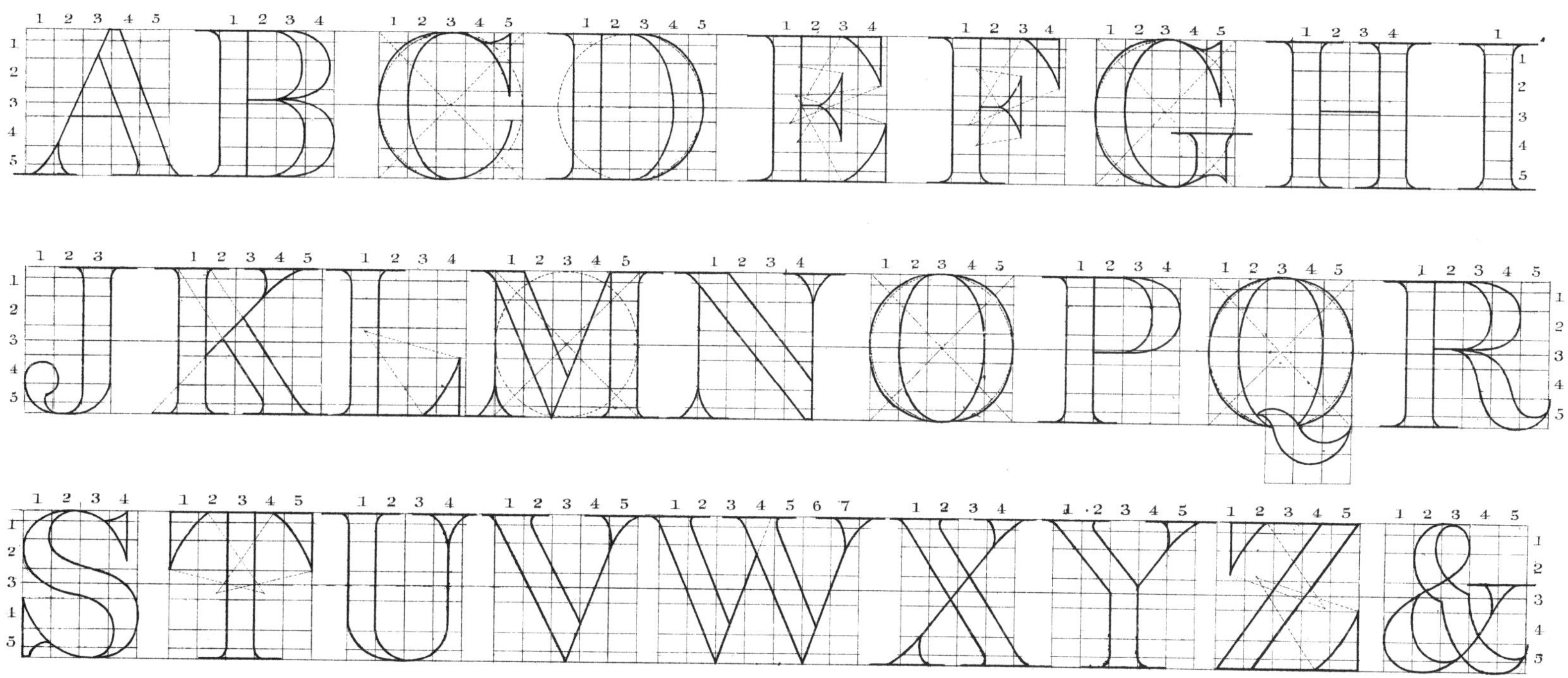

ROMAN SMALL, ANALYTICAL & VARIOUSLY SHADED.

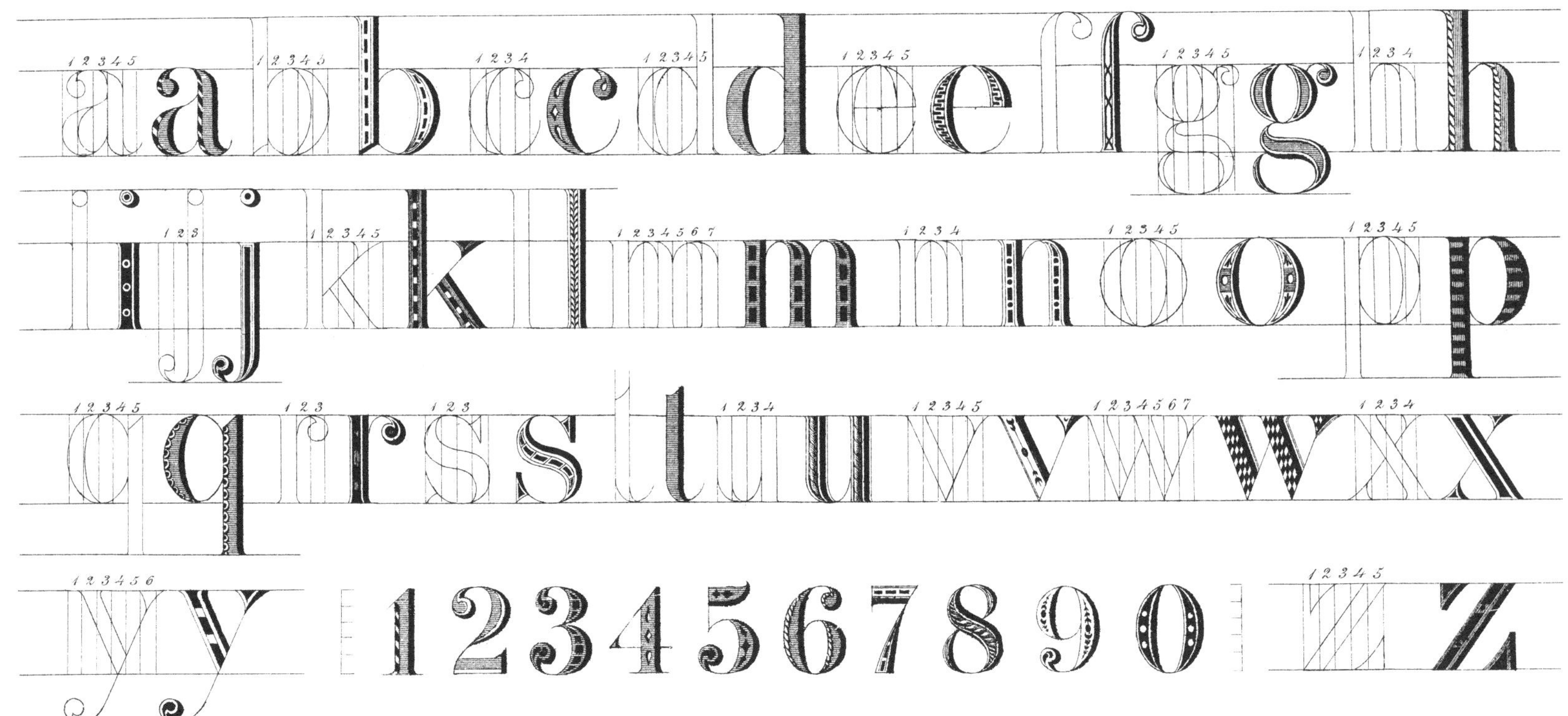

OLD ENGLISH SMALL, ANALIZED.

German Text, Analized.

EGYPTIAN.

ABCDEFGHIJKLMN

OPQRSTUVWXYZ&

abcdefghijklmnopqr

12345 stuvwxyz 67890

SPURRED EGYPTIAN.

BLOCK.

ABCDEFGHIJKLMN

OPQRSTUVWXYZ &

abcdefghijklmnopqr

12345 stuvwxyz 67890

F. S. Copley, Del.

TUSCAN.

ABCDEFGHIJKLMN

OPQRSTUVWXYZ&

abcdefghijklmnopqr

12345 stuvwxyz 67890.

F. S. Copley, Del.

Finished Roman Letters.

ABCDEFGHI

JKLMNOPQR

STUVWXYZ&

Finished Spurred Letters.

SMALL SPURRED ROMAN LETTERS & FIGURES.

abcdefghijklmno

pqrstuvwxyz

1234567890.

Roman Print, Variously Shaded.

A B C D E F G H I

J K L M N O P Q R

S T U V W X Y Z &

PEARL LETTERS.

ABCDEFGHIJ

KLMNOPQRS

TUVWXYZ&.

VELVET LETTERS.

ABCDEFGHI

JKLMNOPQR

STUVWXYZ&

ABCDEFGHIJKLM
NOPQRSTUVWXYZ

abcdefghijklmnopqrs

12345 tuvwxyz 67890

ITALIC.

ABCDEFGHIJKLM

NOPQRSTUVWXYZ&

abcdefghijklmnopqrſstuvvwxyz.

1234567890.

F. S. Copley, Del.

Italic Print, Variously Shaded.

Centre ABCDEFGHIJKLM Line

Centre NOPQRSTUVWXYZ Line

abcdefghijklmnopqrstuvwxyz.

TEXT HAND.

A B C D E F G H I

J K L M N O P Q R

S T U V W X Y Z &

abcdefghijklmnopqrstuvwxyz

1 2 3 4 5 6 7 8 9 0

F. S. Copley. Del.

ITALIAN.

A B C D E F G H I

J K L M N O P Q R

S T U V W X Y Z &

a b c d e f g h i j k l m n o p q r ſ s t u v w x y z z

1 2 3 5 6 7 8 9 0.

F. S. Copley, Del.

OLD ENGLISH.

A B C D E F G H I K

L M N O P Q R S T

U V W X Y Z &.

abcdefghijklmnopqrstuvwxyz

1 2 3 4 5 6 7 8 9 0.

F. S. Copley, Del

A B C D E F G H I K
L M N O P Q R S T
U V W X Y Z &.
a b c d e f g h i j k l m n o p q r s t u v w x y z

F. S. Copley, Del.

GERMAN TEXT.

F. S. Copley, Del.

Aa Bb Cc Dd Ee Ff Gg Hh Ii

Jj Kk Ll Mm Nn Oo Pp Qq

Rr Ss Tt Vv Uu Ww Xx Yy Zz.

1 2 3 4 5 6 7 8 9 0.

F. S. Copley. Del.

German Print.

A B C D E F G H I K

L M N O P Q R S T U

12345 V W X Y Z 67890

a b c d e f g h i j k l m n o p q r ſ s t u v w x y z

F. S. Copley. Del.

14TH CENTURY SMALL (1400)

RICHARD THE SECOND TOMB, WESTMINSTER ABBEY.

15TH CENTURY. (1500)

HENRY VIITHS CHAPEL WESTMINSTER.

A B C D E F G H I K L M N

O P Q R S T U V W X Y Z

a b c d e f g h i k l m n o p q r s t u v w x y z

I + II + III + IV + V + VI + VII + VIII + IX + X +

16TH CENTURY GOTHIC. M. S.

A B C D E F G H I K

I J M N O P Q R S T U

V W X Y Z

GOTHIC, 16 CENTURY.

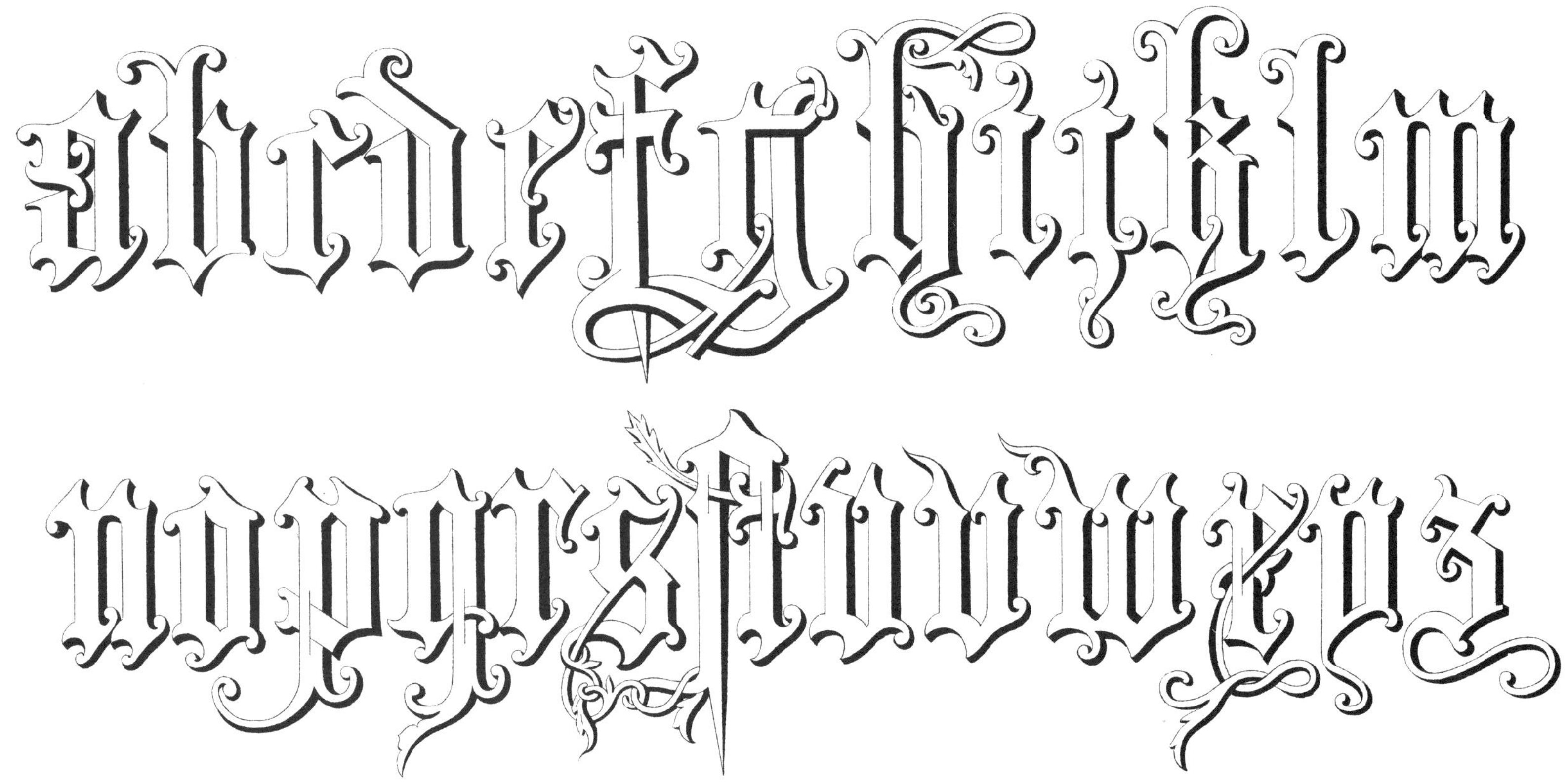

Examples of Ancient Numerals.

12th Century.

1234567890

13th Century.

1234567890

14th Century.

1234567890

1234567890

15th Century.

123456789

1553.

1234567890

16th Century.

1234567890

1617 1673

GREEK.

Αα. Ββ. Γγ. Δδ. Εε. Ζξ. Ηη. Θϑ. Ιι. Κκ. Λλ. Μμ. Νν.

Alpha. Beta. Gamma. Delta. Epsilon. Zeta. Eta. Theta. Iota. Kappa. Lambda. Mu. Nu.

Ξξ Οο. Ππ. Ρρ. Σσς. Ττ. Υυ. Φφ. Χχ. Ψψ. Ωω.

Xi. Omicron. Pi. Rho. Sigma. Tau. Upsilon. Phi. Chi. Psi. Omega.

HEBREW.

י ט ח ז ו ה ד ג ב א

10 9 8 7 6 5 4 3 2 1

Roman Numerals.

I II III IV V VI VII VIII IX X XV XX XXX XL L LX LXX LXXX XC C D M

1 2 3 4 5 6 7 8 9 10 15 20 30 40 50 60 70 80 90 100 500 1000

F. S. Copley, Del.

CIPHERS.

F. S. Copley. Del.

MONOGRAMS.

A.D.1870
R
K
S
L
Charlemagne
Standard of Constantine
Christs Monogram
F.S.Copley.del.

Designs for Flourishing.

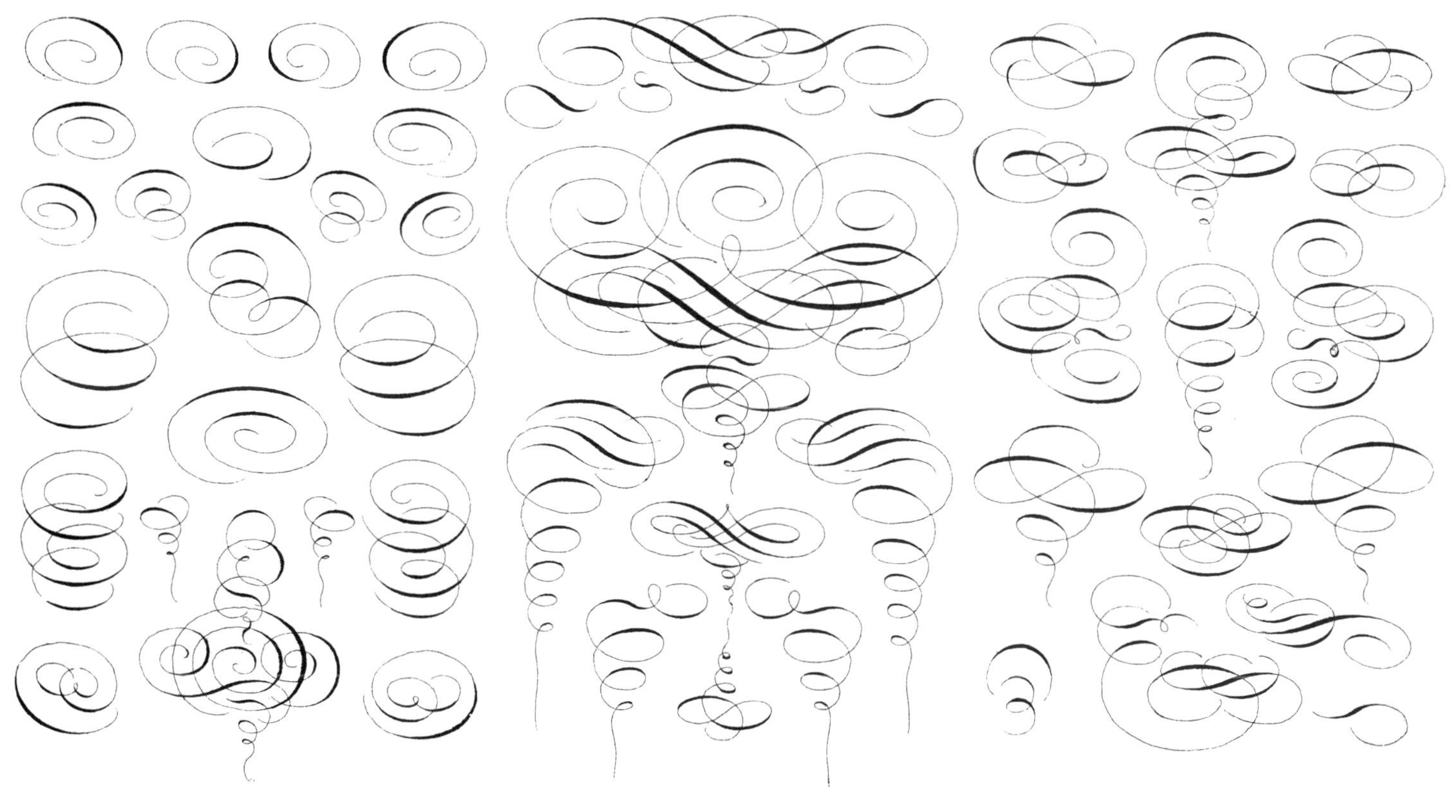

DESIGNS FOR FLOURISHING.

CONSTRUCTION OF TITLES.

THE TRUE METHOD of forming TITLES FOR MAPS, PLANS, &c.

Showing the necessity for construction lines &c.

No. 1.

Original Title		*Model or Trial Title* *Fig. 1.*
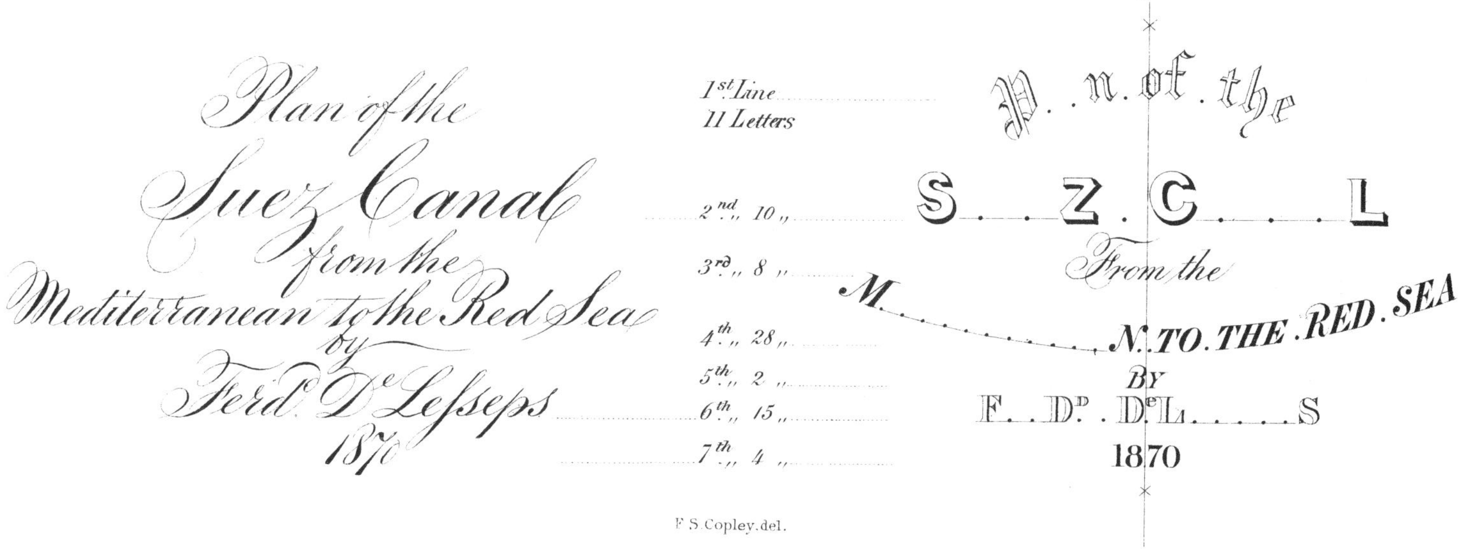 *Plan of the*	1st Line 11 Letters	P . . n . of . the
Suez Canal	2nd " 10 "	S . . . Z . C . . . L
from the	3rd " 8 "	From the
Mediterranean to the Red Sea	4th " 28 "	M . . . . N. TO . THE . RED . SEA
by	5th " 2 "	BY
Ferd. De Lesseps	6th " 15 "	F . . Dd . DeL . . . . . S
1870	7th " 4 "	1870

F. S. Copley. del.

CONSTRUCTION OF TITLES.

No. 2.

NOTE. The Lines drawn thus ———— *represent the construction lines, these Lines should be drawn in Pencil and rubbed out when the Title is finished.*

The Letter I, occupying 2/3rds less space and the Letters M & W 1/3rd more than any other Letter will necessarily throw the middle Letter of a line out of the centre.

F. S. Copley. del.

DESIGNS FOR PORTIONS OF TITLES
FOR MAPS & PLANS.

F.S.Copley.del.

DESIGNS FOR PORTIONS OF TITLES.

FOR MAPS & PLANS.

Section

PLAN OF AN MAP

ESTATE

or

RAILWAY

In the County of

WASHINGTON

SURVEYED

F. S. Copley. del.

EXAMPLES OF TITLES.

LYING NEAR THE DEPOTS
of the
Delaware Lackawanna & Western Railroad,
and the ERIE RAILWAY. 30 Minutes from
NEW YORK.

F. S. Copley. Del

MAP
OF
VILLA SITES
OFFERED FOR SALE
by the
Rutherfurd Heights Association
RUTHERFURD PARK
N.J.

EXAMPLES OF TITLES.

PLAN OF THE

DEPOT GROUNDS AND

Approaches to the

RUTHERFURD PARK STATION

on the

Delaware Lackawanna & Western

RAILROAD

F. S. Copley. Del.

DESIGNS FOR COMPASSES.

F. S. Copley. Del.

Designs for Borders.

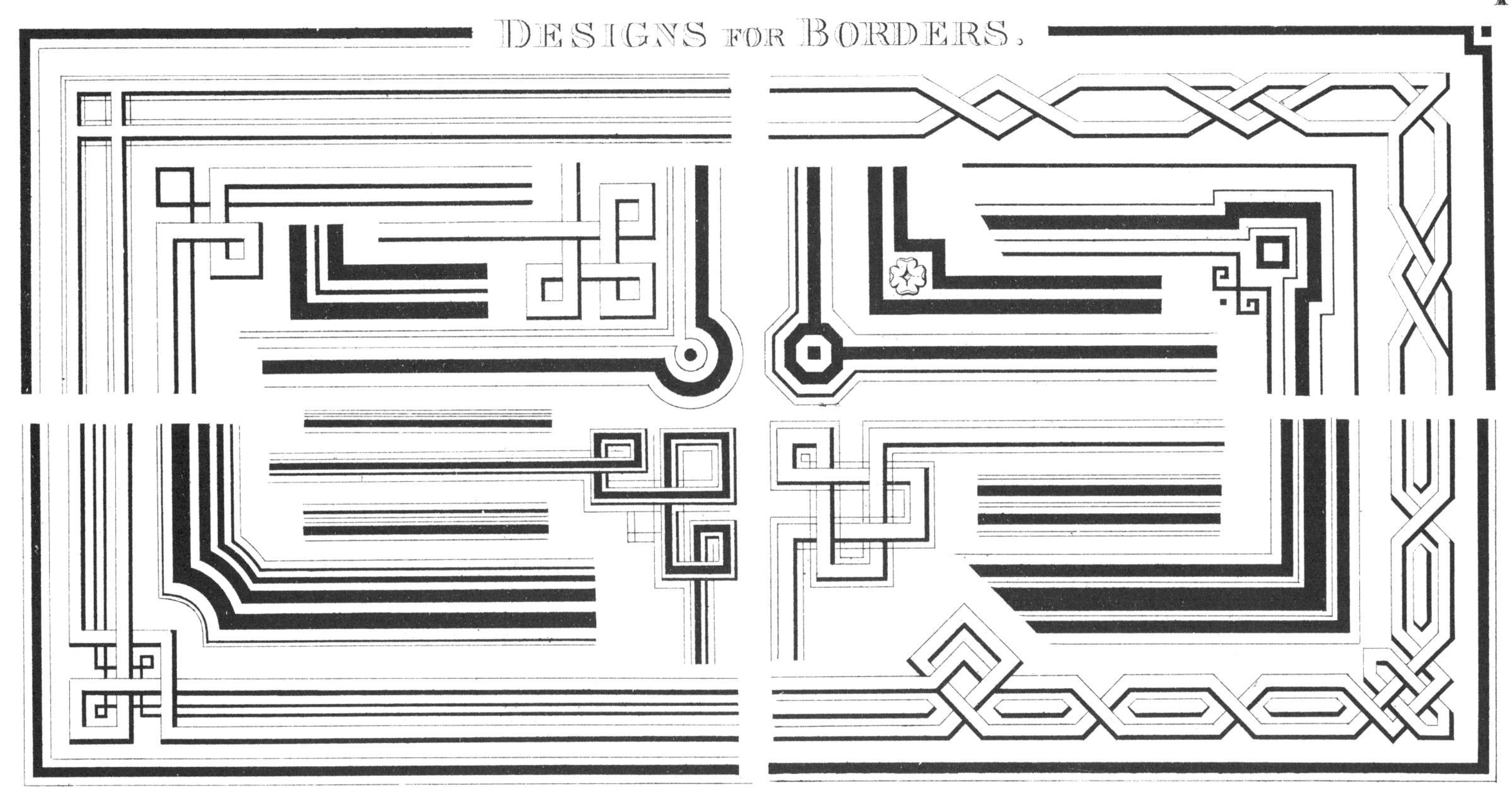

F. S. Copley, Del.

STENCIL PLATES.

Showing the Method of using them.

Fig 5.

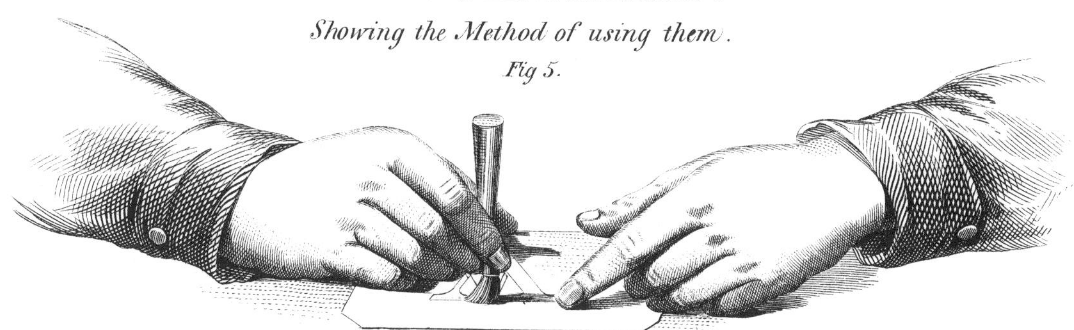

Fig 1.

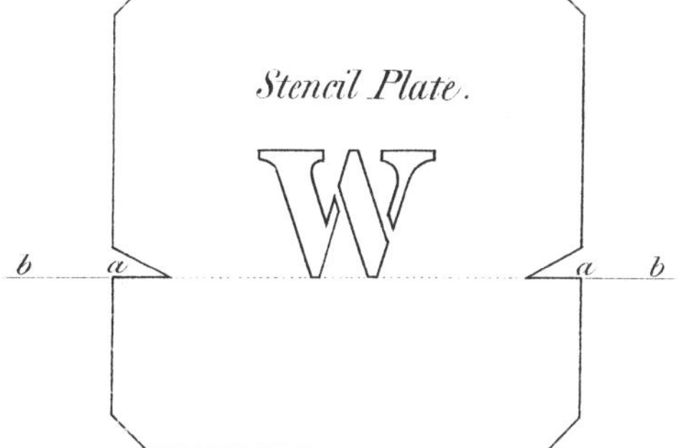

Fig 2.
Impression from

W

Stencil Plate.

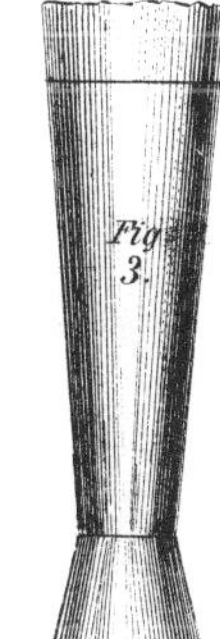

Stencil Plate Brush.

Fig 4.

THE

BOOK OF ORNAMENTAL ALPHABETS;

Ancient and Mediæval,

FROM THE EIGHTH CENTURY

WITH NUMERALS,

INCLUDING

Gothic; Church Text, Large and Small; German Arabesque; Initials for Illumination,

MONOGRAMS, CROSSES, &c.,

FOR THE USE OF

ARCHITECTURAL AND ENGINEERING DRAUGHTSMEN, MASONS, DECORATIVE PAINTERS, LITHOGRAPHERS, ENGRAVERS, CARVERS, &c

COLLECTED AND ENGRAVED BY F. DELAMOTTE.

THIRTEENTH EDITION.

LONDON:
CROSBY LOCKWOOD AND SON, 7, STATIONERS' HALL COURT
1895.

PREFACE TO THE FOURTH EDITION.

AS there are no works of Ancient Alphabets of any excellence published in a cheap form, I have been induced, after many years' study and research in my profession as a Draughtsman and Engraver, to offer this collection to the favourable notice of the public, trusting that its very moderate price and general usefulness will be a sufficient apology for the undertaking.

The demand for a Fourth Edition within so short a period of the publication of the Third, has convinced me in the most agreeable manner that it has been a work required by the public. To render it still more worthy of their attention, I have here introduced some additions, likely to enhance the interest and increase the value of the pages, as an indication of the esteem in which I have held the encouragement, and the respect I have paid to the suggestions of the purchasers of this book, and the critics by whom it has been so liberally reviewed.

INDEX.

8th Century. Vatican.

A B C D E F G H I K

L M N O P Q R S T

V U X Y Z

8th Century. British Museum.

8th and 9th Centuries. Anglo-Saxon.

ABCDEFGHIJ
LMNOPQRS
TUVXZ

9th Century. From an Anglo-Saxon MS. Battel Abbey.

From MS. Library of Minerva, Rome.

10th Century. British Museum.

ABCDEFGHIJ

KLMNNOPQRST

UVXYZ. ÆM

11th Century, and Numerals.

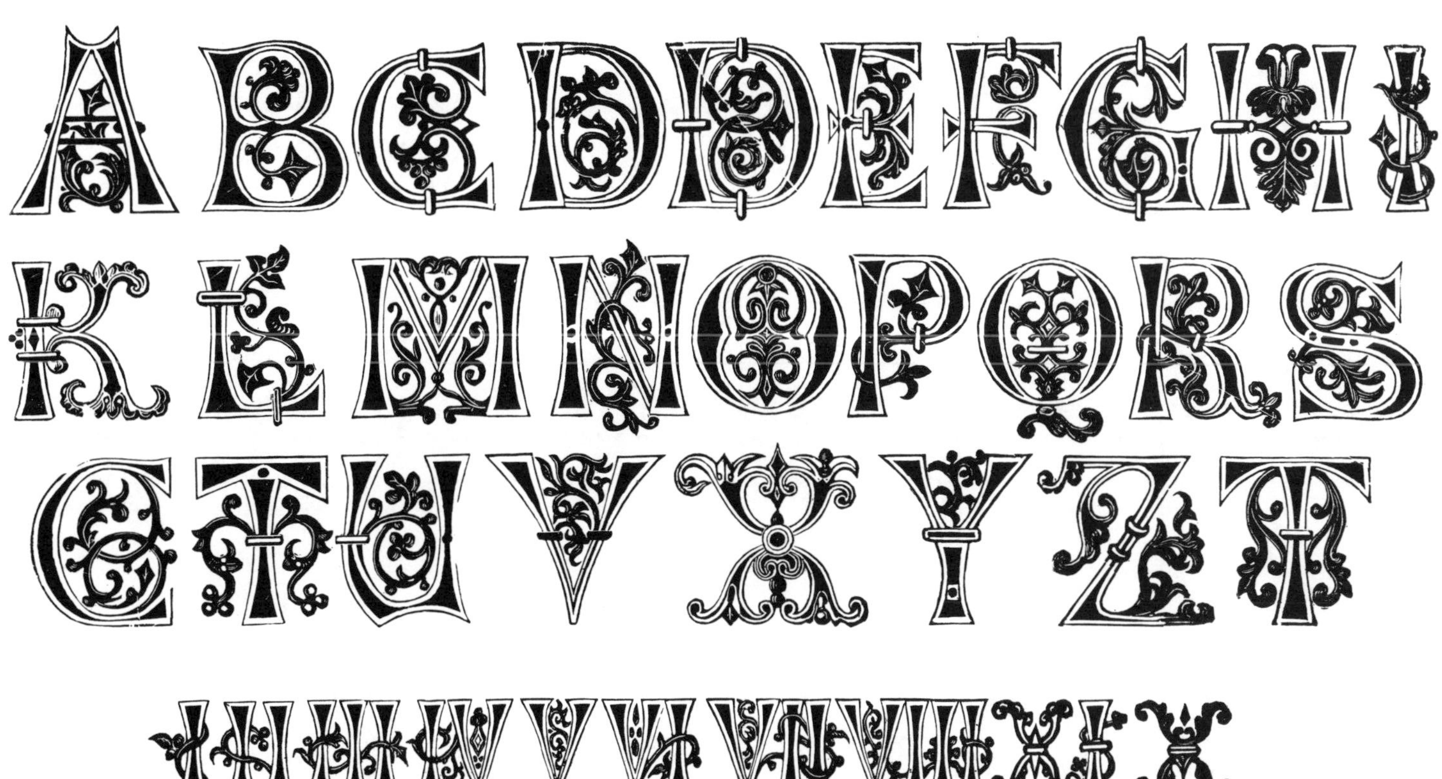

12th Century. From the Mazarin Bible.

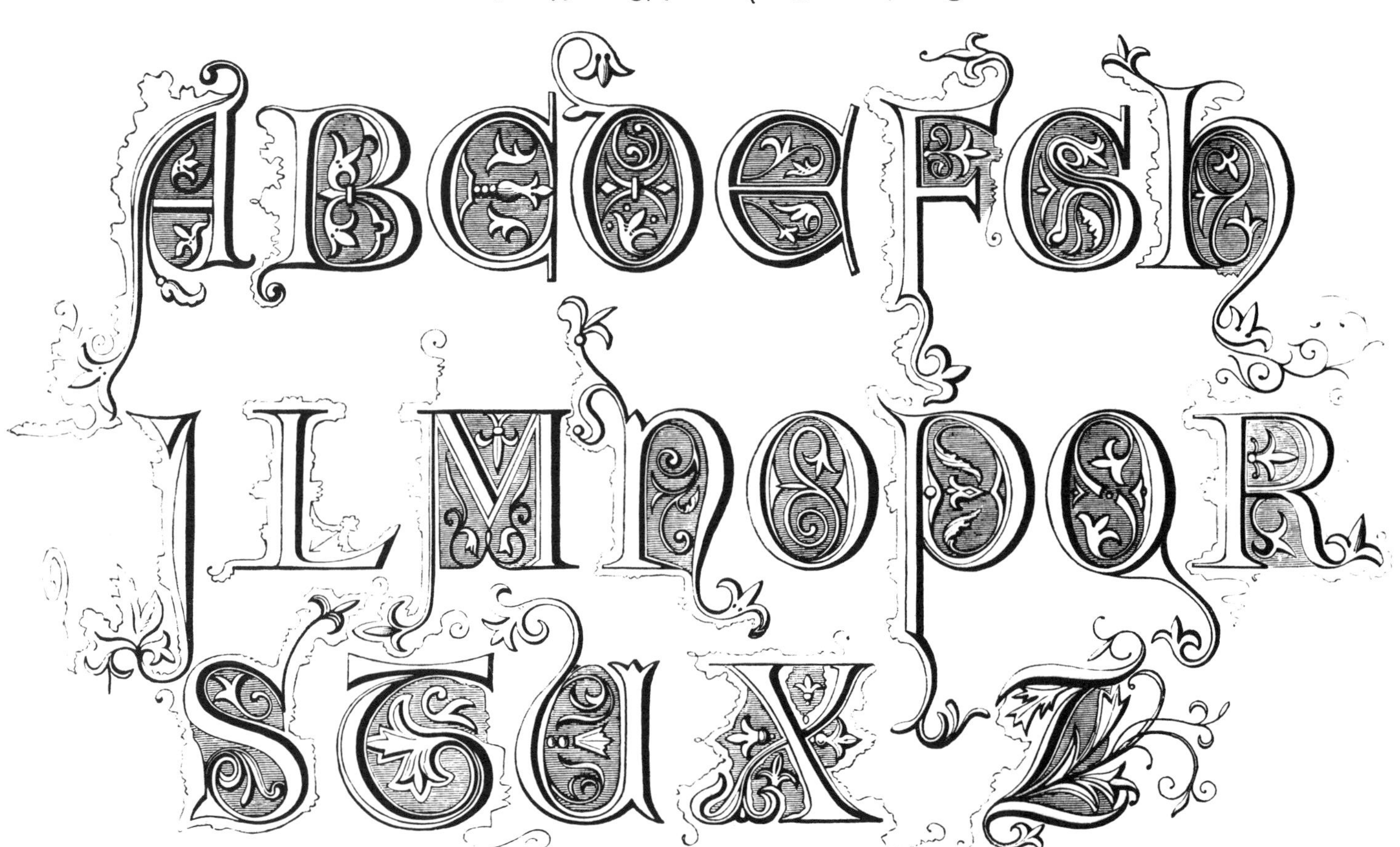

12th Century. British Museum.

a b c d e f g h i k l m n o p q

r s t v w x y z

a a b c d e f g h i k l m n o p q

r t v w x y z

12th Century. British Museum.

ABCDEFGHIJK
LMNOPQRSTU
VWXYZ

12th Century. Bodleian Library.

A B C D E F G H I

K L M N O P Q R S

T U V W X Y Z

13th Century. Henry the Third. Westminster Abbey.

A A B C D E F G
H I K L M N O P Q
R S T U V W X Y Z
T O Z

13th Century. From Latin MS.

13th Century. MS.

ABCDEFGHI
KLMNOPQRS
TUVWXYZ

14th Century. Date about 1340.

ABCDEFGH
IKLMNOPQR
STUVWXYZ

14th Century. British Museum.

14th Century. Illuminated MS.

A B C D E F G H I

K L M N O P Q R S

T U V W X Y Z

14th Century. Richard the Second. 1400. Westminster Abbey.

14th Century. Richard the Second. 1400. Small. Westminster Abbey.

abcdefghiklmnopqrs

tvwxyz.

14th Century. British Museum.

A B C D E F G H I
K L M N O P Q R S
T U V W X Y Z

14th Century. From MS. Munich.

A B C D E F G H I

K L M N O P Q R S

T U V X Y Z

14th and 15th Centuries. Two Small. British Museum.

1475. British Museum.

ABCDEFGH
IKLMNOPQR
STUXYZ

1480. British Museum.

1490. British Museum.

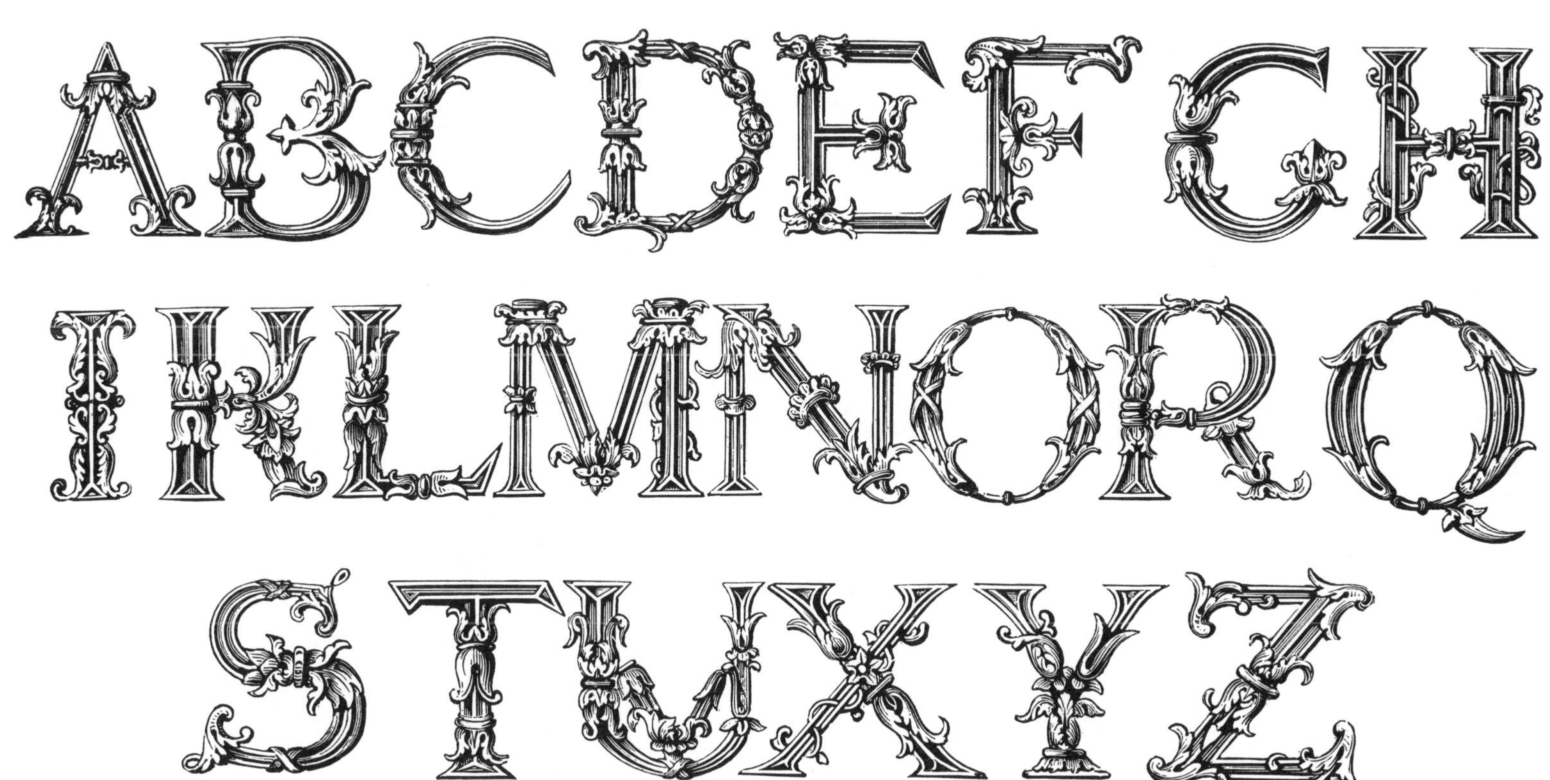

Henry the Seventh. Westminster Abbey.

A B C D E F G H I

K L M N O P Q R

S T V W X Y Z

15th and 16th Centuries. German.

A B C D E F G H I K

L M N O P Q R S T

U V W X Y Z &

15th and 16th Centuries. German. Small.

a a b c d e f g h i j k l m n o p q r

s t u v w x y z

15th and 16th Centuries. Ornamental Riband.

16th Century. Henry the Eighth. MS.

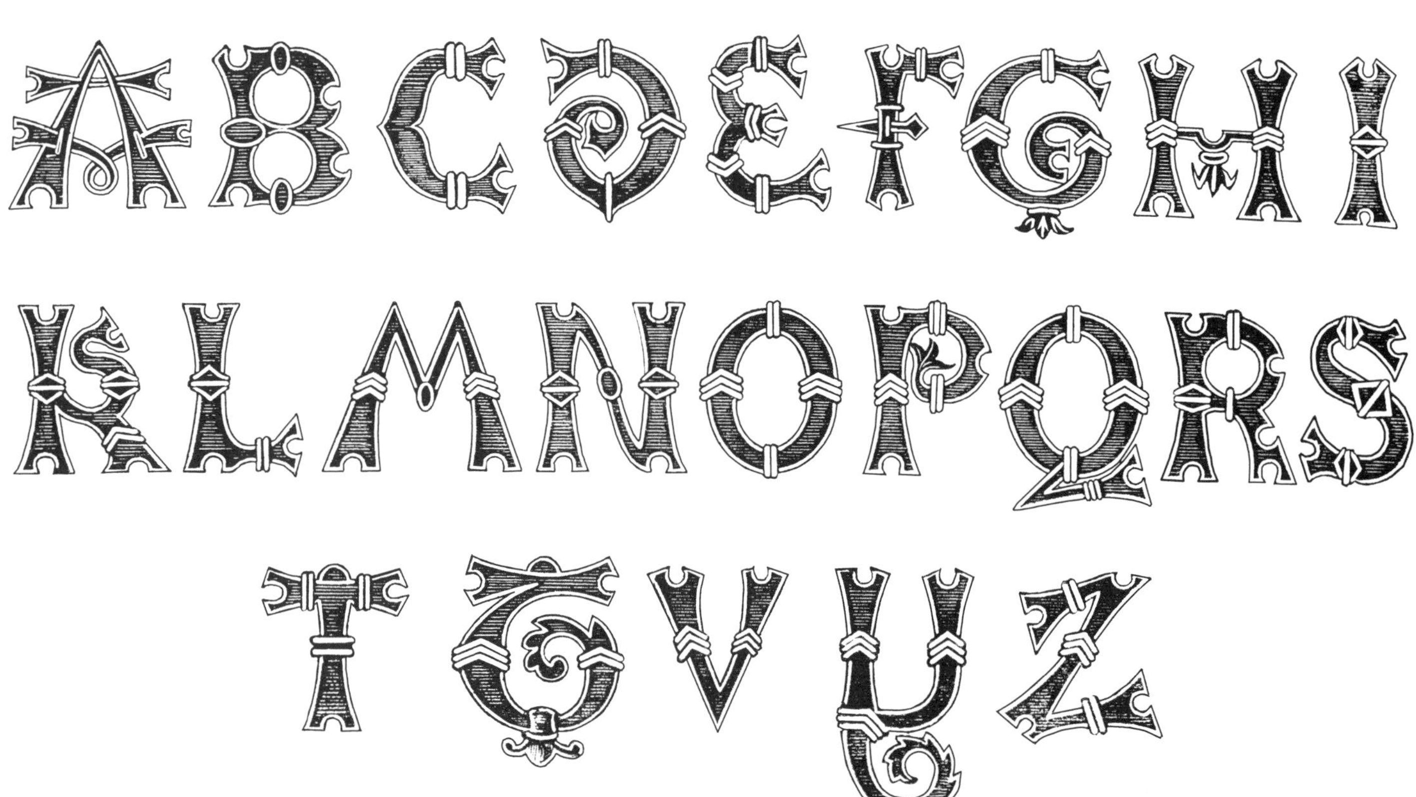

16th Century. From Italian MS.

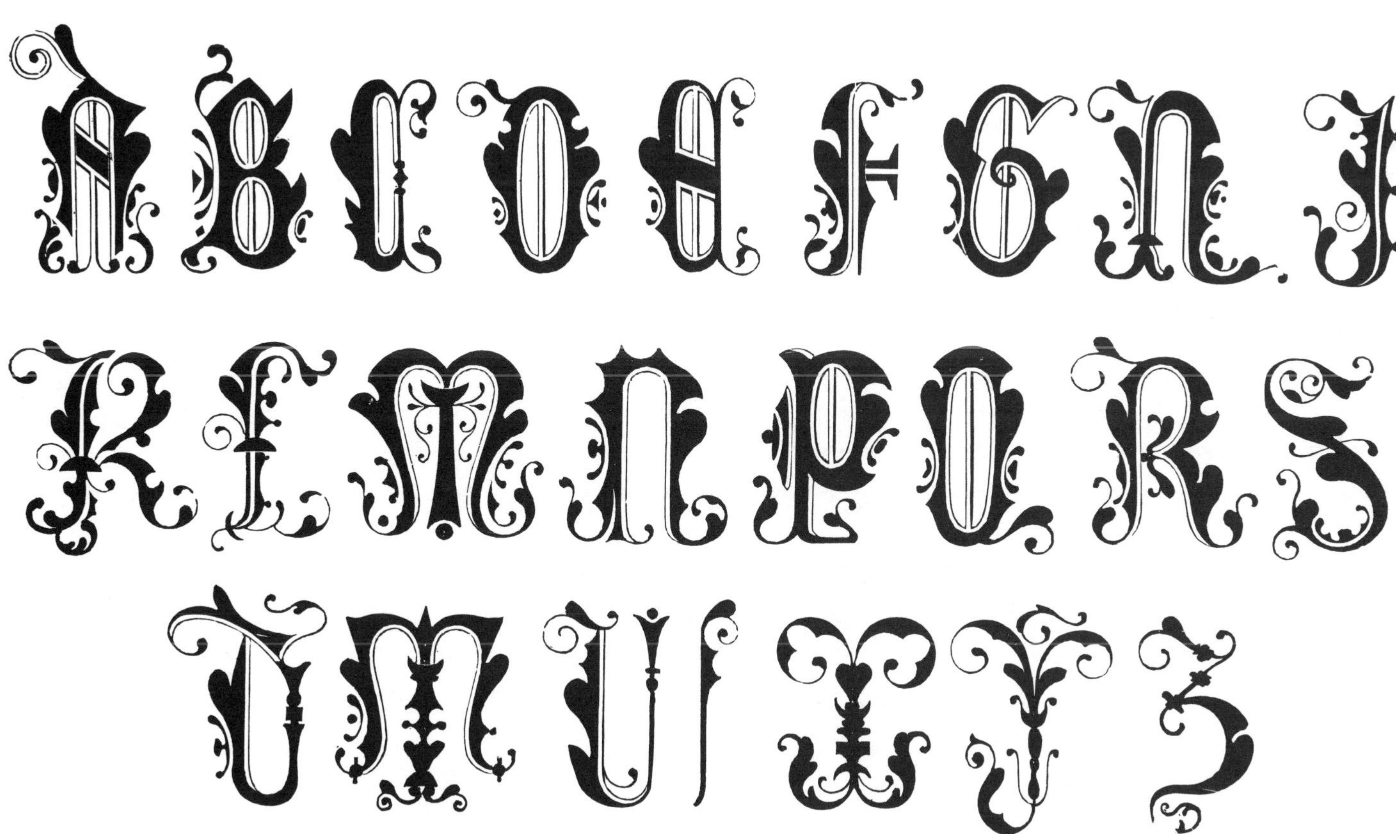

16th Century. Albert Durer's Prayer Book. Lange.

A B C D E F G H

I K L M N O P Q R

S T U W X Y Z

Monogram  1553.

16th Century. Albert Durer's Prayer Book.

abcdefghiklmnopq

rſstuvwxyzzzz

16th Century. Vatican.

16th Century. Gothic. MS.

A B C D E F G H I

K L M N O P Q R S

T U V W X Y Z

16th Century. Gothic.

16th Century. Gothiq MS.

A B C D E F G H I K

L M N O P R S T U V

W X Y Z

16th Century. Large. Small, and Numerals. French. MS.

A B C D E F G H I K

L M N O P Q R S T U V

1 2 3 4 5 W X Y Z . 6 7 8 9 0

b c d e f g h i j k l m n o n q r s t u v x y z z

17th Century. MS.

A B C D E F G H I

K L M N O P Q R S

T U V W X Y Z

17th Century. Church Text. MS.

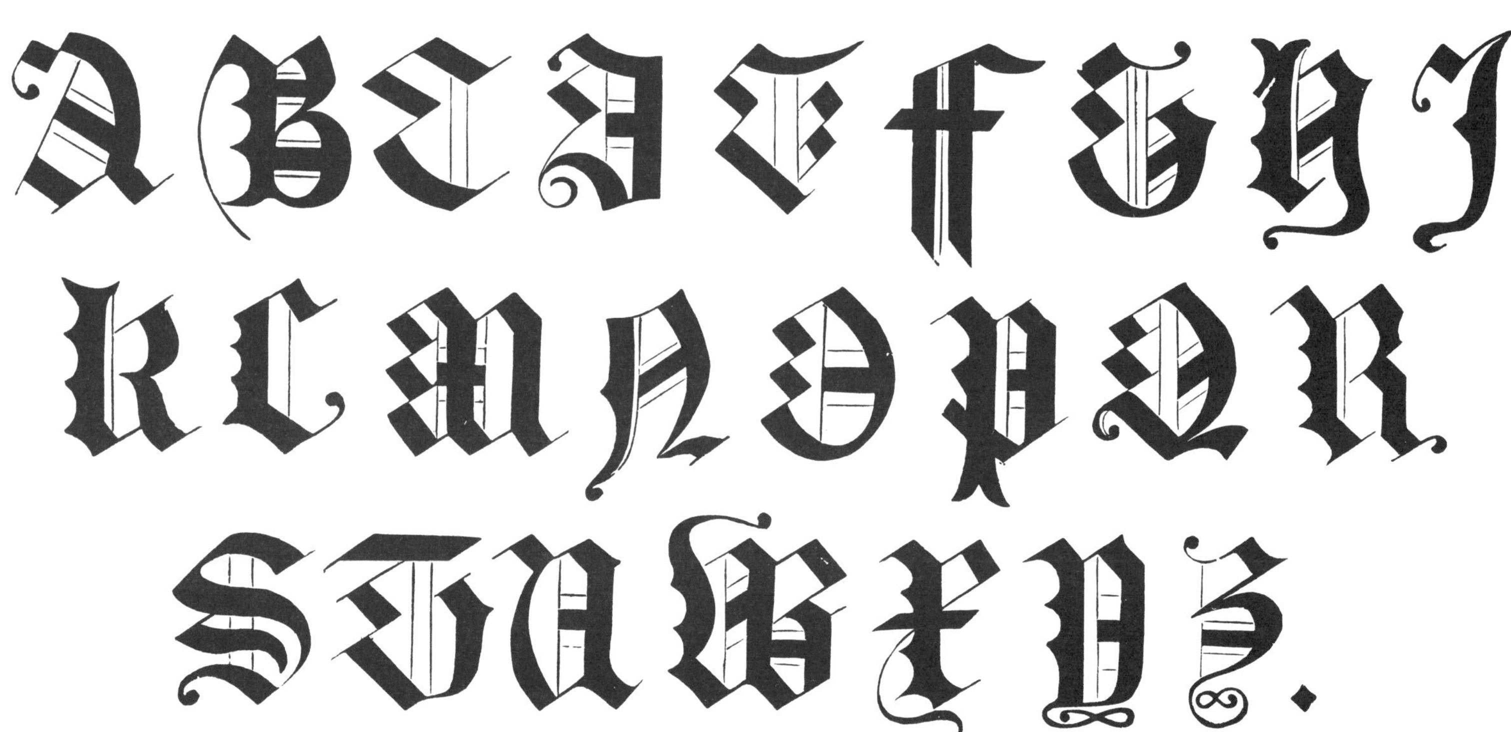

German Arabesque.

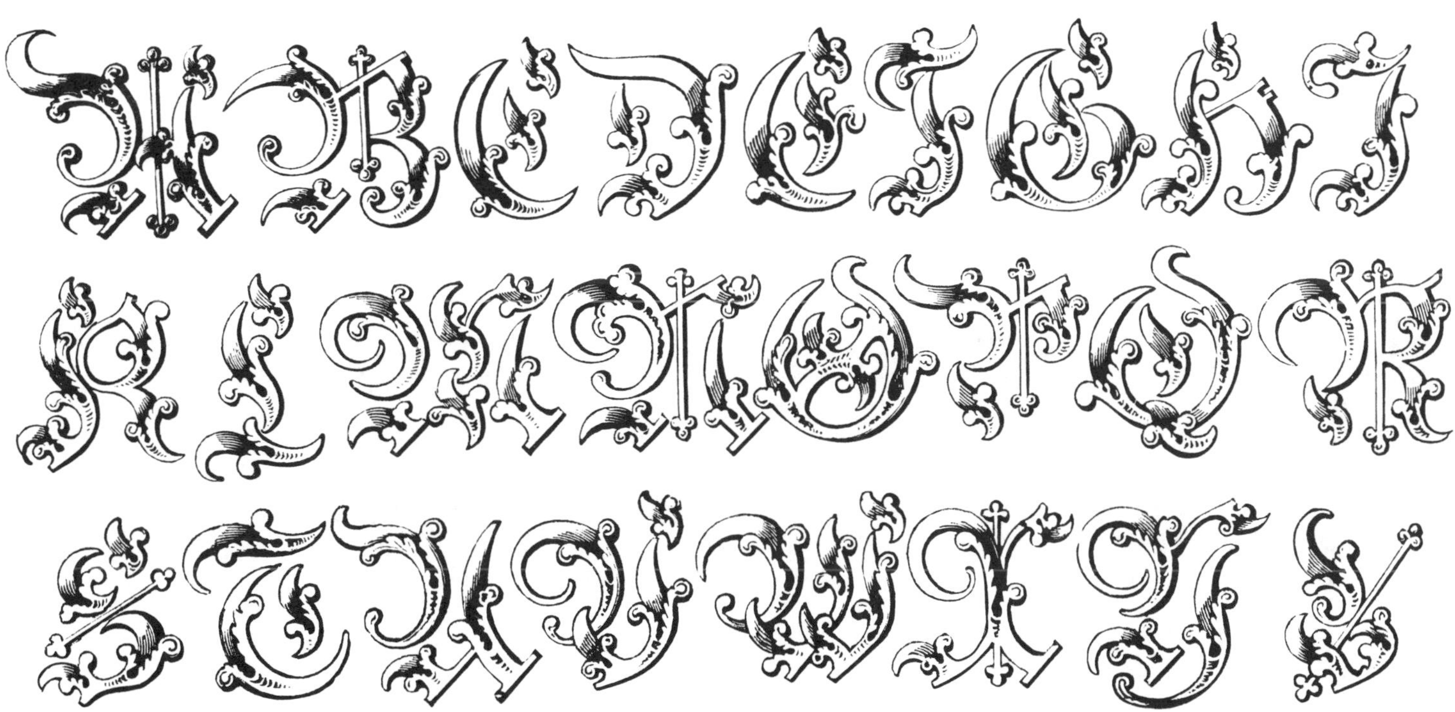

German Arabesque. Small.

Metal Ornamental.

Initials.

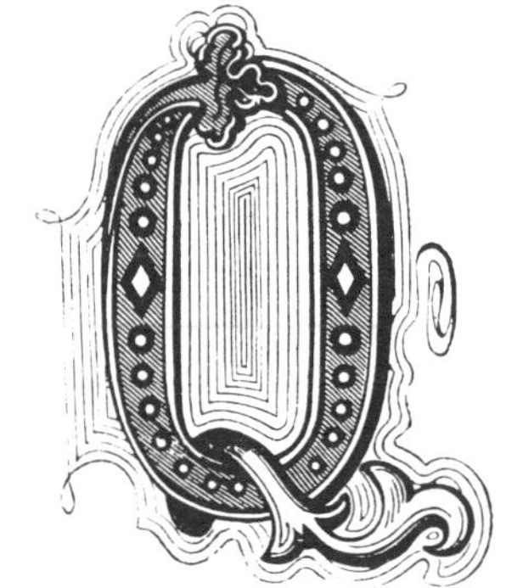

Initials.

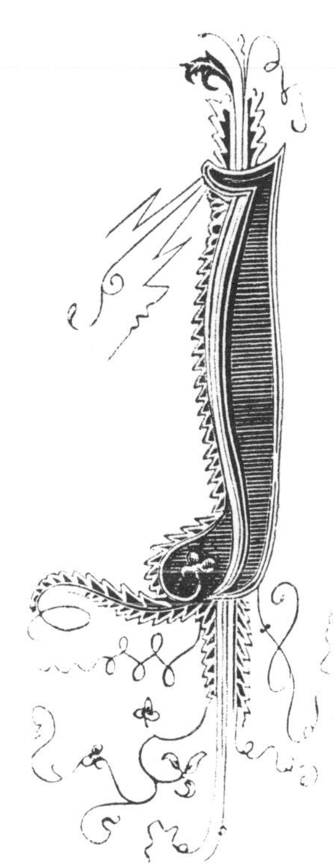

15th Century.

A B C D E F G H K

L M N O P Q R S T U

a b c d e f g h i k l m n o p q r

W s t u v w x y z V

Initials.

Numerals.

9TH CENTURY.

1 2 3 4 5 6 7 8 9 0

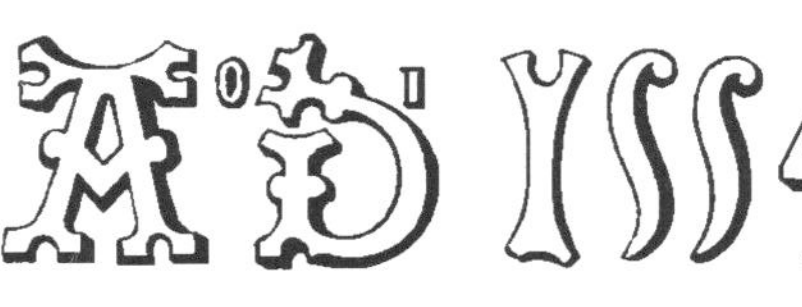

12TH CENTURY.

1 2 3 4 5 6 7 8 9 0

13TH CENTURY.

1 2 3 4 5 6 7 8 9 0

14TH CENTURY.

1 2 3 4 5 6 7 8 9 0

Numerals.

12TH CENTURY

1 2 3 4 5 6 7 8 9 0

GOTHIC.

I + II + III + IV + V + VI + VII + VIII + IX + X

14TH CENTURY.

1 2 3 4 5 6 7 8 9 0

1470.

1 2 3 4 5 6 7 8 9 0

15TH CENTURY.

1 2 3 4 5 6 7 8 9

16TH CENTURY.

1 2 3 4 5 6 7 8 9 0

1553.

1 2 3 4 4 4 5 6 7 7 8 8 9 0

1617 1673

16th Century.

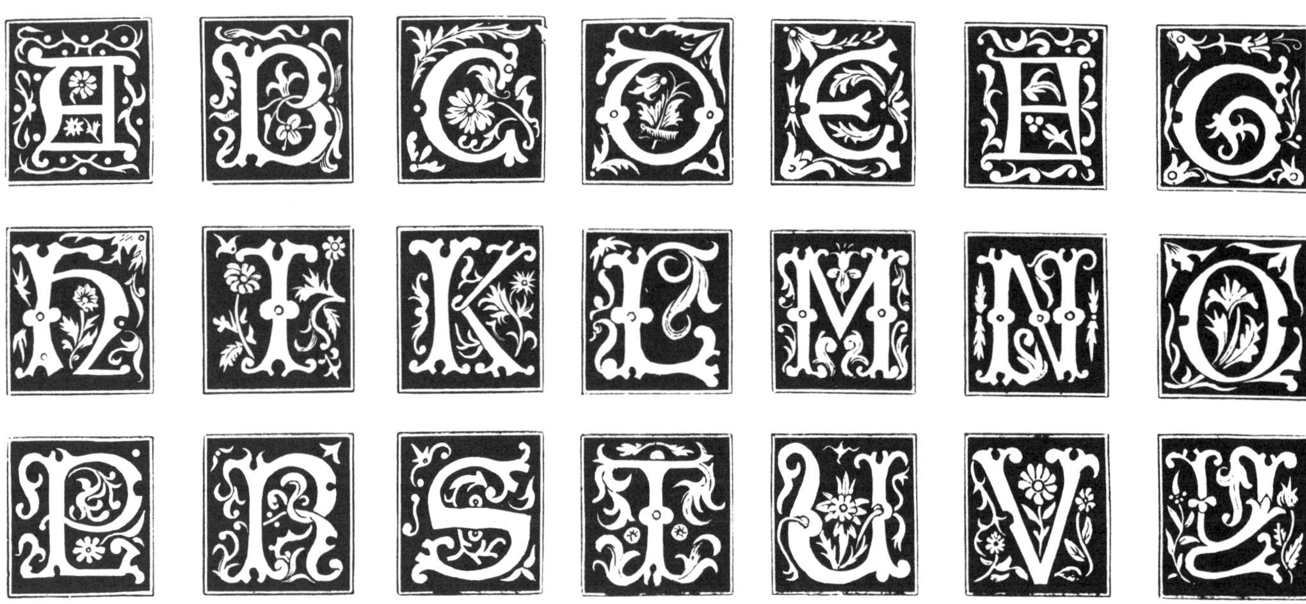

16th Century.

16th Century. From Wood Engravings.

Monograms, Crosses, &c.